W9-CNP-486

The Rush Limbaugh Quiz Book

The Rush Limbaugh Quiz Book

by Ted Rueter

Andrews and McMeel
A Universal Press Syndicate Company
Kansas City

Library of Congress Cataloging-in-Publication Data

Rueter, Ted
    The Rush Limbaugh quiz book / by Ted
Rueter
        p. cm.
      ISBN 0-8362-8099-7
      1. Limbaugh, Rush H.—Miscellanea. I. Title.
    PN1991.4.L48R84 1995
    791.44'028'092—dc20

                                                94-41707
                                                     CIP

Designed by Barrie Maguire

Contents

Acknowledgments

Numerous friends and family members helped me come up with the answers in this book. My gratitude to you all! Thanks also go to my agent, Jane Dystel, and my editor, Donna Martin, for showing so much enthusiasm and for speeding the book to publication. Ryan Coleman provided valuable research assistance, as did Beltway Bob. I am also indebted to Jeremy Solomon and Ken Brady, authors of *The Dan Quayle Quiz Book*, for blazing the trail. And thanks to Rush for providing so much material!

Introduction

Rush Limbaugh is everywhere. His radio show, heard on more than six hundred stations, reaches more than twenty million listeners a week. His daily television program is on more than 220 stations, and trails only "Late Show" and "Nightline" in the late-night ratings. His two books, *The Ways Things Ought to Be* and *See, I Told You So*, have sold more than seven million copies. His "Rush to Excellence Road Show" has played in ninety cities, with crowds as large as seven thousand people. His newsletter, *The Limbaugh Letter*, has more than 430,000 subscribers.

And the world has taken notice. Rush has been on the cover of *Time, US News and World Report, The New Republic, National Review,* and *The American Spectator*, and has been the subject of a *Playboy* interview. He has appeared on David Letterman, MacNeil-Lehrer, "20/20," "Nightline," "Meet the Press," and "Donahue." Barbara Walters calls Rush "the most controversial man in America."

There's little doubt that Rush has staying power. Some political analysts suggest that he could be a presidential candidate in 1996. In the words of the *Boston Globe*, "Rush Limbaugh is not disappearing any time soon, that's for sure."

Readers of this book will learn all sorts of fun and useful information about Rush, such as:
—what he did for fun as a teenager
—his idea of a perfect weekend
—his romantic involvements
—his philosophical agreement with Woody Allen
—his fantasies
—his aversion to self-promotion and braggadocio
—his proposal for "The Homeless Olympics"
—his thoughts on the most beautiful thing about trees

—his views on Bill, Hillary, Al, Anita, and Ted
—his opinions on condoms, feminazis, peace
   pansies, and lesbians.

No red-blooded, patriotic American should be without this book. In the "Era of Limbaugh," it is every citizen's duty to learn as much as possible about "the most dangerous man in America."

I. THE EARLY RUSH

Rush Limbaugh has always had a high opinion of himself. He told *Playboy* in December 1993 that "from the time I was six years old, I have known that I was going to do something, whatever it was, with fame and notoriety. I've never, ever doubted that. It got me through a lot of the dark days. I always knew it was going to happen. Always."

So what sort of dark days were there for young Rush? Well, how about dropping out of college, being fired six times, two failed marriages, having to live with his parents in his twenties, and making $12,000 a year at the age of 28? Peter J. Boyer, in *Vanity Fair*, describes the young Rush as "a pudgy kid with a flat-top who craved popularity but never penetrated the in-crowd." Novelist D. Keith Mano notes that Rush "majored in failure as a young man."

Things started turning around for Rush in 1983, when he got a talk show at KFBK-AM in Sacramento. After being a "big whale in a little pond" for five years, Rush went national. On August 1, 1988, "The Rush Limbaugh Show" premiered with fifty-six stations and 250,000 listeners. Rush was on his way toward his goal of being the best radio talk show host of all time.

But how much do you really know about the early Rush? Do you know his real name, his childhood nickname, his pranks as a disc jockey, his childhood idol, his duties with the Kansas City Royals, and what he did for fun as a teenager? Take the first part of the quiz and find out.

1. What was one of the favorite pastimes of Rush's father?

   a. telling Rush that he was going to be a big-time failure

   b. driving down Main Street in Cape Girardeau, Missouri, busting mail boxes with a baseball bat

   c. breaking Rush's piggy bank and using the money to play the slot machines in Kansas City

   d. tackling antiwar protesters and cutting their hair with pruning shears

   e. yelling at Walter Cronkite during the evening news

2. What was Rush's nickname as a high school football player?

   a. Blimpmeister

   b. Benchwarmer Bob

   c. The Crusher

   d. Rush the Toe

   e. Rocko

3. Whom did Rush replace at KFBK-AM in Sacramento?

   a. Venus Flytrap

   b. Morton Downey, Jr.

   c. Paul Harvey

   d. John McLaughlin

   e. Arthur Godfrey

4. What is Rush's real name?

   a. Bryant Gumbel

   b. Rush Hudson Limbaugh III

   c. Jeff Christie

   d. Randall Ulysses Hampton

   e. Rushford Benjamin Limbaugh

5. At radio station KMBZ in Kansas City, Rush constantly received memos from the management for "demeaning and sexist behavior toward his female co-anchor." What was Rush's offense?

   a. He played with her hair while reading the news.

   b. He always asked her about her previous evening's activities after doing the weather.

   c. He constantly called her "lovely and gracious."

   d. He frequently referred to her as his "co-anchorette."

   e. He repeatedly opened the program by telling her that she reminded him of his mother.

6. What was Rush's nickname as a kid?

   a. Wallywomp

   b. Rusher

   c. Hounddog

   d. Rusty

   e. Big Guy

7. What course did Rush fail his freshman year at Southeast Missouri State?

   a. Introduction to Speech

   b. American Government

   c. Introductory Economics

   d. Ballroom Dancing

   e. Afro-American History

8. Of what magazine did Rush's dad say, "It might as well be printed in Russia. It's equivalent to *Pravda*"?

   a. *National Geographic*

   b. *Playboy*

   c. *Time*

   d. *Socialist Review*

   e. *Reader's Digest*

9. What were Rush's responsibilities with the Kansas City Royals?

    a. organize Coca-Cola Sports Wallet Day, Yago Ladies Shoulder Bag Day, Hostess Cake Helmet Day, Coors Seat Cushion Day, and Kodak Camera Day

    b. usherette

    c. political education of leftfielders

    d. singing the "Star Spangled Banner"

    e. third base coach

10. Why was Rush fired by WIXZ-AM in Pittsburgh?

    a. for using the word "bugger"

    b. for playing "Under My Thumb" by the Rolling Stones too many times

    c. for calling George McGovern a "militant vegetarian antinuke bean-curd eater"

    d. for encouraging his listeners to deposit their garbage on the front lawn of the mayor's house

    e. for renting a helicopter and bombing the Pinedale Shopping Mall with turkeys

11. Which of the following pranks did Rush *not* pull as a disc jockey in Pittsburgh?

    a. He told his listeners that he had a picture phone and could see everything they were doing.

    b. He promised to give five thousand dollars to the fifth caller without getting permission from the station manager.

    c. He attempted to purchase slacks with a left-handed zipper from a discount clothing store.

    d. He called a sporting goods store and placed an order for a left-handed bat.

    e. He attempted to rent flash bulbs from a camera store.

12. Who was Rush's idol as a kid?

    a. Karl Marx

    b. Spiro Agnew

    c. Winston Churchill

    d. Babe Ruth

    e. Larry Lujak

13. What did Rush do for fun as a teenager in Cape Girardeau, Missouri?

   a. He didn't.

   b. He was a member of the high school pom-pom team.

   c. He conned people by pretending to be running the Baptist Church's "Know Your Bible" contest.

   d. He broke into the high school chemistry lab and stuck frogs and lizards in the experiments of his girlfriend, Suzy Farcus.

   e. Each Saturday, he visited the town fortune teller, Madam Whitlock, who told him, "You have talent on loan from God."

14. What did Rush wear to a St. Patrick's Day parade in Sacramento?

   a. his birthday suit

   b. Ross Perot ears

   c. jogging shorts and a UCLA sweatshirt

   d. a bullet-proof vest

   e. a porkie hat, black leather jacket, white T-shirt, and motorcycle boots

15. What television programs did Rush watch regularly with his second wife?

   a. "Married With Children" and "A Current Affair"

   b. "Nightline" and "This Week with David Brinkley"

   c. "Oprah" and "Geraldo"

   d. "Wheel of Fortune" and "Jeopardy"

   e. "All My Children" and "Dallas"

16. What did Rush do at the wedding reception for his friend, Kansas City Royals baseball player George Brett?

   a. He sang a special song for the couple that had been written by a mutual friend.

   b. He mooned an AIDS protester who had crashed the party.

   c. He fell into a drunken stupor and admitted that he had voted for Walter Mondale in 1984.

   d. He led a recitation of "The Pledge of Allegiance."

   e. He set up a booth to sell "dittohead" T-shirts.

17. Where did Rush and his second wife get married?

   a. at the Taj Mahal

   b. in the Lincoln Bedroom at the White House

   c. at a banquet room at Royals Stadium

   d. at the Vatican

   e. at the studios of the Excellence in Broadcasting Network

18. How would Rush respond when asked if he and his second wife were going to have any kids?

   a. "Well, let's see how she does with the dogs first."

   b. "I love babies. It's teenagers I can't stand."

   c. "What if it's a girl?"

   d. "Not until they develop a vaccine for liberalism."

   e. "Of course. My sperm is on loan from God."

19. What job did Rush's grandfather have in the Eisenhower administration?

   a. liaison to Senator Joseph McCarthy

   b. minister of propaganda

   c. director of the Belgian Endive Promotion Board

   d. ambassador to India

   e. golf caddie to the president

20. What position was Rush's uncle appointed to by President Reagan?

   a. presidential nap-time coordinator

   b. astrological adviser to Nancy Reagan

   c. sexual harassment adviser to Clarence Thomas

   d. personal representative to the Evil Empire

   e. a federal judgeship

21. What school did Rush's first wife graduate from?

a. Slippery Rock State College

b. Pepperdine University

c. the Ted Baxter Famous Broadcasters School

d. the Weaver Airline and Personnel Training School

e. the Elkin Institute of Radio and Technology

22. What conflict did Rush face with his second wife's family?

a. He insisted on playing a tape of his radio show any time they were together in a car.

b. They were nudists.

c. They believed in the Peace Corps, unions, and John Kennedy.

d. They were members of the Nation of Islam.

e. They believed that Flipper the dolphin was smarter than Rush. Rush would respond, "Could someone please show me one hospital built by a dolphin?"

23. What problem did Rush's brother David have with his sixth grade teacher?

a. He demanded that the teacher shave his mustache, in order to "look like an American."

b. He tried to force the teacher to teach the theory of evolution.

c. He constantly told the teacher that his brother Rush "had talent on loan from God." The teacher always responded, "God is dead."

d. Each morning, he tried to conduct an in-class prayer in support of J. Edgar Hoover's campaign against homosexuals.

e. He accused the teacher of communism, for wanting to give everyone equal grades.

24. What was one of the reasons Kansas City Royals baseball player George Brett enjoyed being friends with Rush?

a. "The guy was always willing to go out for pizza and beer."

b. "Whenever I would buy something, like an answering machine or a VCR, I didn't know how to hook it up, and so I would call Rush to come over and do it."

c. "He knew how to hit left-handed pitching."

d. "He gave me tips on seducing women."

e. "He was a pinball wizard."

25. How did Rush learn about dating?

    a. He once hid himself in the backseat of a car so he could steal a peek when a friend necked with his date.

    b. He read *How to Win Friends and Influence People*, by Dale Carnegie.

    c. He watched reruns of "The Andy Griffith Show," to see how Barney Fife made the moves on Thelma Lou.

    d. In high school, he took a class on "Marriage and the Family," where he wrote a thirty-five-page paper on "The Role of Male Supremacy in the Development of Western Civilization."

    e. He purchased an instructional video by Alan Alda.

II. THE PERSONAL RUSH

Rush has clearly made it big—but is he happy? For
one thing, he seems to have problems relating to
women. His first two marriages ended in divorce.
Rush got married the first time because "I was doing
what I thought I had to do." His second marriage
failed after he moved to New York and didn't have
time for his wife.

Part of Rush's problem with women may be his atti-
tude. He refers to radical feminists as "feminazis" and
female reporters as "reporterettes" and "info-babes." In
his book *See, I Told You So,* Rush says that "the fine
art of seduction" is now "being confused with sexual
harassment."

Alas, on May 28, 1994, Rush walked down the aisle
for the third time. He met his wife, Marta Fitzgerald,
through CompuServe, the on-line information service.
Fitzgerald wrote to Rush in 1990, asking how to react
to a Reagan-bashing professor at the University of
North Florida. Rush initially failed to respond.
Fitzgerald then wrote a second letter, criticizing him
for expressing interest in meeting some flight atten-
dants who had written him. Fitzgerald called him a
pompous fool who was wasting his time. One of
Fitzgerald's ex-husbands commented, "That's how the
whole relationship started. They started corresponding
back and forth."

Rush's wedding took place at the home of Supreme
Court Justice Clarence Thomas, who officiated. After
the ceremony, the men retired to a separate room,
where they smoked cigars.

This section of the quiz is about Rush's personal
life, including his family, his favorite movie, his military record, his drug usage, his prescription for personal success, and his idea of a great weekend. Keep
working at the quiz—and remember, no cheating.
Because Rush wouldn't want you to.

26. According to Rush, "I don't particularly like
_____."

    a. meeting new people

    b. liberals

    c. sex. It's so messy

    d. Jack Kemp. His voice drives me crazy

    e. going to sleep. You never know what stunts Bill and Hillary are going to pull in the middle of the night

27. What is Rush's principal hobby?

    a. placing late-night phone calls to members of the National Organization for Women

    b. blowing smoke in Ted Kennedy's face

    c. raking leaves

    d. reading romance novels

    e. watching pro football on television

28. Rush's favorite restaurant in Kansas City is the renowned Stroud's. Why does Rush love the place?

    a. "They serve Florida orange juice with every meal."

    b. "They refuse to serve broccoli, out of respect for President Bush."

    c. "It's nothing fancy. Pan-fried chicken, gravy and mashed potatoes."

    d. "I can smoke my cigar in the men's room."

    e. "I always pay with a check, and they've never cashed one of them."

29. Where does Rush live?

    a. in Connecticut, next door to David Letterman

    b. in the studios of the Excellence in Broadcasting network

    c. in New Jersey, with his mother

    d. in a small apartment on Manhattan's ultraliberal Upper West Side

    e. in a house on Long Island he shares with Debra Winger

30. Which three people from all of history would Rush bring with him to a desert island?

   a. Jesus Christ

   b. Newton

   c. Mussolini

   d. Helen Keller

   e. Abraham Lincoln

   f. Joan of Arc

   g. Plato

   h. Mimi Rogers

   i. Thomas Jefferson

31. What is Rush's favorite movie?

   a. *Mr. Smith Goes to Washington*

   b. *Bedtime for Bonzo*

   c. *Debbie Does Dallas*

   d. *Rambo*

   e. *Love Story*

32. According to Rush, "I melt around _____."

   a. little dogs

   b. Marilyn Quayle

   c. young Republicans in cheerleader outfits

   d. my mother

   e. pints of Ben and Jerry's

33. Whom has Rush expressed a desire to meet?

   a. Nancy Reagan

   b. Joan Lunden

   c. Fidel Castro

   d. Jimmy Swaggart

   e. Tammy Faye Baker

34. How did Donna Dees, Rush's former girlfriend (and a publicist for Dan Rather), defend her romantic involvement with Rush?

   a. "He pays for everything."

   b. "He's the best kisser this side of Buffalo."

   c. "Right-wing demagogues turn me on."

   d. "The man opens doors and loves his mother. What more do you want?"

   e. "He is not the Antichrist that my feminist friends paint him as."

35. According to Rush, "I never owned _____."

   a. a box of Bungee condoms

   b. a copy of *Mein Kampf*

   c. a pair of blue jeans

   d. an AK-47

   e. a driver's license

36. Rush once lost sixty pounds in six weeks. How did he do it?

   a. nonstop sex with the Pointer Sisters

   b. eating nothing but vitamin pills and grapefruit juice

   c. liposuction

   d. having himself frozen

   e. round-the-clock coaching by Richard Simmons

37. Who was Rush's date when he accompanied President and Mrs. Bush to the Kennedy Center in 1992?

   a. Cindy Crawford

   b. Senator Nancy Kassebaum

   c. Whoopi Goldberg

   d. Fawn Hall

   e. Roger Ailes

38. How old was Rush when he registered to vote?

   a. 18

   b. 21

   c. 25

   d. 35

   e. Rush refuses to vote, since "it only encourages them."

39. How many times has Rush smoked marijuana?

   a. never

   b. once, and his mother made him write a note of apology to President Eisenhower

   c. twice, and it made him nauseous

   d. four times, with Bill Clinton, Al Gore, Bruce Babbitt, and Douglas Ginsburg

   e. every day, because he's at his best when he's high

40. What is Rush's military record?

a. He was a member of the Green Berets in Vietnam, where he killed thirteen Viet Cong with his bare hands.

b. He served in a Marine unit with Gomer Pyle.

c. He was classified 4-F after a physical found an "inoperable pilonidal cyst" and "a football knee from high school."

d. He made military training films in Hollywood.

e. He fled to Canada, where he worked for seven years as a bouncer at "La Girl Femme."

41. What is Rush's prescription for personal success?

a. keep getting fired

b. flunk out of college

c. get divorced twice

d. keep gaining weight until you've hit 320 pounds

e. "No matter what your status in life, you can learn about what's possible for you in this country by studying me."

42. Why was Michelle Sixta, Rush's second wife, initially attracted to him?

a. "I could tell he had talent on loan from God."

b. "It was exciting because I was used to dating college-age guys who didn't have any money. If they took me out, it was for pizza, and a lot of times, I paid. They didn't have a car."

c. "He never stopped talking. There was never a lull in the conversation."

d. "He loved my cooking."

e. "He did a great Ross Perot impersonation."

43. What were Rush's plans after he was fired by the Kansas City Royals?

a. open a roadside café outside Albuquerque

b. run for mayor of Rio Linda, California

c. become a professional wrestler

d. "I was seriously thinking of going to work for Guy's Foods, a potato chip company in Liberty, Missouri. I was going to sell potato chips, not drive the route truck. I was going to be a management guy for $35,000 a year. I was looking at that as Nirvana."

e. become the anchor of "Action News" in Grand Island, Nebraska

44. Who was Rush's first client as a corporate spokesman in Sacramento?

  a. the California Alliance for Motherhood

  b. the Reagan presidential library

  c. Dairy Queen

  d. General Electric

  e. Nutri System

45. What is Rush's view of a perfect weekend?

  a. traveling through Utah in a beat-up van listening to the Grateful Dead

  b. not getting dressed, not leaving his apartment, ordering takeout for all his meals, listening to music, and reading

  c. listening to tapes of "The Best of Rush"

  d. hosting a dittohead convention

  e. appearing on "Meet the Press" and attending a Pittsburgh Steelers game

46. What does Rush's mom think of his success?

   a. She's embarrassed as hell.

   b. She's put him up for adoption.

   c. She's built a "Rushstock" museum in the basement of her house.

   d. She can't get over the fact that a guy who couldn't find a date in high school and flunked out of college has amounted to anything.

   e. She has called him numerous times to express her happiness, except for the time she chastised him for saying that Amy Carter was ugly.

47. With whom has Rush been romantically linked?

   a. Madam Hollywood

   b. Dame Edna Ethridge

   c. Connie Chung

   d. Julia Roberts

   e. Princess Diana

48. What does Rush think "are just a tremendous addition to the enjoyment of life"?

   a. condoms

   b. cigars

   c. all-you-can-eat pizza places

   d. older women

   e. foot massages

49. Appearing as himself on "Hearts Afire," what words of endearment did Rush offer to a female character?

   a. "Hey, baby. Wanna know what I'm real liberal about?"

   b. "You smell as good as a Cuban cigar."

   c. "She puts the 'fem' in feminazi."

   d. "You look like the sort of woman who's nice even when she's got PMS."

   e. "I bet you're as smart as Hillary."

50. After the 1992 election, Rush stayed overnight in the Lincoln Bedroom of the Bush White House. He wrote a note to television producers Harry Thomason and Linda Bloodworth-Thomason, who were scheduled to stay in the same room the night of Clinton's inauguration. What did the note say?

a. "You people are from Arkansas? What a bunch of hicks! That state's nothing but a collection of alligator farms and junkyards."

b. "Can I get on 'Hearts Afire'?"

c. "I was here first, and I will be back."

d. "Hey, Harry—I've heard you've got a little travel agency. Why don't you get your friend Bill to fire the entire White House travel office and have him send some business your way?"

e. "Linda Bloodworth-Thomason? What kind of woman hyphenates her last name? Are you some sort of feminazi?"

III. RUSH THE HUMANITARIAN

This section is called "Rush the Humanitarian" in recognition of the fact that Rush loves people. Who but an altruist:

—would call Roger Clinton "the president's half-witted half-brother"?

—would refer to Rio Linda, California, as the city where they "place a six-pack in the tomb of the unknown bowler"?

—would urge George Bush to conduct a "liberal outing" of Bill Clinton?

—would refer to the dead as having "assumed room temperature"?

—would argue that "America is being held hostage by Clintonistas"?

—would tell a reporter, "You're trying to establish that I'm a bigot, Nazi-racist pig"?

In this chapter, learn how Rush uses his warm, friendly, gentle humor on his favorite people. Be thrilled as Rush comes up with titles for movies on Anita Hill. Chuckle as Rush tells you what he thinks of Al Gore. Find out who Rush thinks is "the queen of political correctness." Be mesmerized by Rush's thoughts on the best job for Ted Kennedy. Commit to memory what Rush said after homeless advocate Mitch Snyder committed suicide. Absorb Rush's view of Gorbachev's distinguishing feature as a Soviet leader. Master what Rush said about Madonna's book, *Sex.*

And keep this in mind: Rush is documented to be right 97.9 percent of the time.

51. When someone suggested that Supreme Court Justice David Souter was "in the closet," Rush said, "I think any of us would be safer in a closet with David Souter than _____."

    a. a woman would be in an office with Clarence Thomas

    b. a straight guy would be taking a shower in President Clinton's army

    c. a Jew would be in Nazi Germany

    d. a white guy would be in South Central L.A.

    e. we would be in an automobile with Ted Kennedy

52. What does Rush call former New York governor Mario Cuomo?

    a. "Mr. Mafioso"

    b. "Mario Coomo"

    c. "that Italian guy"

    d. "America's biggest crook since Jimmy Hoffa"

    e. "Mr. Big Mouth"

53. Which of the following descriptions of Ross Perot did Rush *not* make?

   a. "the little general"

   b. "a hand grenade with a crewcut"

   c. "He'd have followers even if he were in a strait-jacket in a padded cell."

   d. "Ross 'I'm all ears' Perot"

   e. "a weird little runt"

54. What did Rush say upon the opening of Woody Allen's film *Husbands and Wives*?

   a. "Husbands and wives? I'm not qualified to comment."

   b. "Divorce, promiscuity, May/December romances, love triangles: it's liberalism in action, folks."

   c. "Gee, I hope it's rated PG so Woody can bring a date."

   d. "Woody Allen is the poster boy for the Democratic party."

   e. "I never go to movies. None of the seats are big enough."

55. What does Rush call Ronald Reagan?

   a. "Ronald the Magnificient"

   b. "Attila the Hun"

   c. "Gramps"

   d. "Ronaldus Magnus"

   e. "Bonzo"

56. What was Rush's comment after murderer-cannibal Jeffrey Dahmer pleaded innocent by reason of insanity?

   a. "That's like finding William Kennedy Smith guilty of rape and then having a trial to see if he was horny."

   b. "Innocent by reason of insanity? With that kind of logic, millions of liberals should be rotting in jails."

   c. "I'm sure this makes Mary Jo Kopechne feel much better."

   d. "Only in Milwaukee. That place is so cold it destroys brain cells."

   e. "Life itself is insane. I was reading Jean-Paul Sartre this weekend, and I'm experiencing existential angst big time."

57. According to Rush, "I have a lot of friends who are _____."

 a. Mormons

 b. dolphin-hugging wacko environmentalists

 c. male lesbian lotsa drummers

 d. long-haired, maggot-infested, dope-smoking peace pansies

 e. liberal, commie bastards

58. Which of the following is *not* a title Rush suggested for a movie on Anita Hill?

 a. *Driving Miss Sleazy*

 b. *I Wish I Had Three Men and a Baby*

 c. *Desperately Seeking Clarence*

 d. *Sex, Lies, and Anitagate*

 e. *From Smear to Eternity*

59. What did Rush say about Al Gore?

    a. "He's a bona fide tree-hugging, spotted owl–loving, snail-darter-protecting, Gaia-worshiping, radical doomsday prophet."

    b. "Nothing but a stiff, pseudo-intellectual techno-twit."

    c. "The guy couldn't dance his way out of a hoolahoop. I mean, did you see him at the Inaugural Ball? I heard Tipper had to see a podiatrist for a month!"

    d. "He's got the soul of a vice president."

    e. "Gore has proven that the vice presidency's worth a warm bucket of spit."

60. Which of the following statements has Rush *not* made about Bill Clinton?

    a. "I do not make ad hominem attacks on Clinton. They all deal with policy—or character."

    b. "The most politically incorrect president since Franklin Roosevelt."

    c. "Robo-Candidate"

    d. "He's the dope from Hope."

    e. "Bill Clinton lies brazenly. Then he lies brazenly to cover his brazen lies. Then he lies brazenly to cover his brazen cover."

61. Rush plays the following song, "The Philanderer" (sung to the tune of "The Wanderer"), on his radio show:

> Oh, well I'm the type of guy who would never
>   settle down
> Where pretty girls are, well you know that
>   I'm around
> I kiss 'em and I love 'em cause to me they're
>   all the same
> I get so gosh darned hammered, I don't even
>   know their name
> 'Cause I'm a philanderer, yes a philanderer
> I sleep around, around, around, around,
>   around

Whom do the lyrics refer to?

a. Gary Hart

b. Clarence Thomas

c. Robert Packwood

d. Joey Buttafuoco

e. Ted Kennedy

62. Match Rush's description with the appropriate individual:

a. "the queen of political correctness"

1. Lloyd Bentsen

b. "marvels at the wonders of Eastern European–style central planning and collectivism"

2. David Gergen

c. "the next surgeon general in the Clinton administration"

3. Anita Hill

d. "My guess is she's had plenty of spankings"

4. Donna Shalala

e. sings "Algorean chants to Mother Earth"

5. Carol Browner

f. "the Cadaver"

6. Laura D'Andrea Tyson

g. "Sleazer of the House"

7. Janet Reno

h. "In New Jersey, _____ is a prom date"

8. Jim Wright

i. "Lord Bentsen"

9. Alan Cranston

j. "David Rodham Gergen"

10. Jack Kevorkian

63. What job does Rush think would be appropriate for Ted Kennedy?

    a. commissioner of Little League baseball

    b. towel attendant at Burning Tree Country Club

    c. corporate spokesman for Weight Watchers

    d. ruler of the Soviet Union

    e. trial attorney for victims of sexual harassment

64. When homeless activist Mitch Snyder committed suicide and a note was found, what did Rush say?

    a. "There but for the grace of God go I."

    b. "Another one bites the dust."

    c. "I wonder if I was mentioned."

    d. "The revolutionary vanguard of the proletariat—it's gone."

    e. "Nah nah nah nah, nah nah nah nah, hey hey, good-bye."

65. In Rush's view, who are Jerry Brown's core supporters?

   a. "environmental wackos and multiculturalists"

   b. "Jane Fonda and Ted Turner"

   c. "rich Democrats who are on the payroll of Communist organizations"

   d. "spaced-out Hollywood actors who eat beans and rice"

   e. "every freak and kook organization that gravitates toward the Democratic party"

66. According to Rush, what is Bill and Hillary's objective in domestic policy?

   a. to create a "paternalistic utopia" of family-leave bills, minimum-wage legislation, comparable-worth laws, affirmative-action plans, and child-protection laws

   b. "to hasten the international Communist revolution"

   c. "to tax and spend the United States into bankruptcy"

   d. "to force all men to receive training in hugging and crying"

   e. "to require corporations to fire all Republicans"

67. Which of the following has Rush *not* said about Hillary Clinton?

    a. "What a cutie! That layout in *Vogue* was a real turn-on."

    b. "Hillary abruptly changed her image, hair style and all, from harridan to homemaker, for the balance of the campaign."

    c. "an antiwar activist extraordinaire"

    d. "co-president"

    e. "the smartest woman to ever walk the face of the earth"

68. In 1984, what did Rush do on his radio show to illustrate presidential candidate Gary Hart's "new ideas"?

    a. He played Art Garfunkel's rendition of "Don't Know Much About History."

    b. He did an hour-long interview with Donna Rice.

    c. He offered thirty seconds of silence.

    d. He conducted the program from "The Monkey Business" off the coast of Bimini.

    e. He read from *The Communist Manifesto*.

69. According to Rush, "The only difference between Gorbachev and other Soviet leaders is that _____."

    a. he's got this birthmark. It seems to be growing in typical Soviet expansionist fashion. Right now you can see Florida, the Gulf of Mexico, the tip of Texas, Chappaquiddick, and Kennebunkport

    b. Gorbachev is alive

    c. his wife has nice legs

    d. he understands English

    e. Gorbachev didn't threaten to nuke us

70. What did Rush say about Madonna's book, *Sex*?

    a. "Given the controversy raging in the New York public school system regarding sex instruction, I think they've found their first-grade textbook."

    b. "I didn't know half that stuff."

    c. "Sex? I'd rather not talk about it."

    d. "Who'd want to look at hundreds of nude pictures of Madonna? I mean, if it was Dolly Parton, sure—but *Madonna*?"

    e. "My book, *The Way Things Ought to Be*, was always ahead of *Sex* on the best-seller lists. I've always been on top of Madonna, as it were. Ha, ha, ha."

71. Where does Rush place himself ideologically?

   a. "on Ronald Reagan's lap"

   b. "just to the right of Benito Mussolini"

   c. "in bed with Phyllis Schlafly and Marilyn Quayle"

   d. "sandwiched between Pat Buchanan and Jerry Falwell"

   e. "in the Bennett/Kemp/Limbaugh wing of the Republican party"

72. What did Rush have to say about the "Year of the Woman"?

   a. "Those bitches want everything."

   b. "Anything to make Hillary and Tipper happy."

   c. "Carol Mosely Braun claimed during the campaign that women are better equipped than men to 'nurture' the economy back to health. What are you going to do, Senator Braun—*breast-feed* it?"

   d. "I'm sure glad I'm not married."

   e. "It's always women this, women that. When is it going to be the 'year of the *man*'?"

73. Whom has Rush called "great"?

   a. Dan Quayle

   b. Oliver North

   c. Mother Teresa

   d. Charles Barkley

   e. Jack Kemp

74. What did Rush say after Madonna's Florida home was wrecked by Hurricane Andrew?

   a. "I'm sure the neighbors are happy."

   b. "It's not the first time some guy has blown into town, trashed her, then left her in the morning."

   c. "I wonder if she was wearing clean underwear."

   d. "I hope none of her boy-toys were damaged."

   e. "Somebody call the cops! The NAACP is sure to organize a looting expedition!"

75. What does Rush call the Clinton administration?

   a. "the best thing that's happened to my career since Ross Perot"

   b. "Slick Willie and the Razorbacks"

   c. "the Raw Deal"

   d. "the biggest collection of far-out leftists and closet socialists this side of Havana"

   e. "the Billary Hour"

IV. RUSH ON POLITICS

Like it or not, Rush Limbaugh is a major player in American politics. He endorses candidates, he gets into fights with presidents, he stays overnight at the White House, he reprimands the American public for its frequent "Gorbasms," and he focuses public attention on issues such as "Whitewatergate" and "Fornigate." Rush could strongly influence the 1996 Republican presidential nomination by issuing an endorsement.

Rush supported Pat Buchanan for president during the 1992 Republican primaries. Buchanan, elated, promised to name Rush his White House communications director (which, in Rush's view, would clearly have been a step down).

During the spring and summer of 1992, Rush was appalled at the fact that many of his listeners supported Ross Perot. Rush regarded Perot as a fraud, and referred to him as "that little guy."

Bill Clinton's election as president was a great boon for Rush's career. Instead of having to defend his pals George Bush and Dan Quayle, he suddenly had a great new target. While Rush supported Clinton on the NAFTA treaty, most of his comments have been merciless.

Clinton and Rush even engaged in a public, personal battle. Speaking at Washington's famed Gridiron Club, Clinton cited Rush's defense of Attorney General Janet Reno after she was treated rudely by Congressmen John Conyers at a hearing on the Waco disaster. Clinton joked, lamely, that "the only reason Rush Limbaugh was defending her was that she was attacked by a black guy." While Rush loves calling other people "environmental wackos" and "closet socialists," he protested that Clinton's name-calling hurt his feelings.

44

Rush's views on politics have attracted loads of attention. *Newsweek* calls Rush "the last angry white man" and "the American White Male under siege." A *Boston Globe* reporter wrote that Rush "is to deep thinking what Roseanne Barr is to serious acting: funny, wildly popular, and vacuous," and that he is what cheese puffs are to real food: "nearly addictive, gobbled up by almost everyone, but a nutritional zero."

More charitably, a Bible study group at the First Assembly of God in Charlotte, North Carolina, concluded (after ten weeks of study) that Rush's views adhere to Christian teaching. While the group didn't approve of Rush's cussing, they gave him high marks for truth, opposition to abortion, criticism of the press, and advocacy of spiritual awakening.

Rush has even attracted scholarly attention. Daniel J. Evearitt, a professor of religion and theology at Toccoa Falls College in Toccoa Falls, Georgia, is the author of *Rush Limbaugh and the Bible*. While Evearitt believes that Rush's dogma is largely consistent with biblical teaching, he also cautions Christians against attaching their faith "too closely to any person, any political party, or any agenda."

In addition, Philip Seib, a professor of journalism at Southern Methodist University, wrote *Rush Hour: Talk Radio, Politics, and the Rise of Rush Limbaugh*. Seib argues that Rush "is part of a long tradition of radio masters—politicians such as Franklin Roosevelt and Huey Long, and entertainers such as Arthur Godfrey and Jack Benny."

This portion of the quiz tests your knowledge of Rush's views on politics. A true Rushophile should know Rush's opinions on condoms, feminazis, Dan Quayle, liberals, gays, the New Left, the homeless, nuclear weapons, the animal rights movement, blacks, environmentalism, the poor, NAFTA, trees, health care, women in the military, and the Clinton administration. Do you qualify?

45

76. Appearing as himself on "Hearts Afire," Rush said he was willing to make one exception to his opposition to women in military combat. What is it?

a. "I say there ought to be equal military opportunity for feminazis. Buy them all a one-way Greyhound ticket to North Korea."

b. "I'd make an exception for Madonna. Those steel-cup bras are really missile launchers."

c. "Roseanne Arnold. She's scary enough to make anyone surrender."

d. "Except for Lorena Bobbitt. Give her a bayonet and send her out ten minutes ahead of the other guys."

e. "With the exception of anyone named 'Pat' or 'Tracy' or 'Chris.' A girl should have a girl's name, not a boy's name."

77. What does Rush have to say about the civil rights movement?

    a. "When are those people going to stop whining and get a job?"

    b. "They're nothing but a bunch of house niggers."

    c. "I told this black guy he was a credit to his race, and he got all upset. What's with those people?"

    d. "Pretty soon they're going to start demanding their own country. Fine. Good riddance. Let them have Cleveland."

    e. "It is neither farfetched nor unfair to draw an analogy between the civil rights leadership and the Soviet Communist leadership, insofar as exploitation of their people is concerned."

78. What does Rush call San Francisco?

    a. "the West Coast branch of the Kremlin"

    b. "left coast city"

    c. "Sodom and Gomorrah"

    d. "a prophylactic paradise"

    e. "AIDS City"

79. According to Rush, what is the goal of animal rights activists?

   a. "To force parents to name their daughters 'Bambi.'"

   b. "They want the extermination of the human race."

   c. "To make sure everyone eats nothing but bananas, frozen yogurt, and bagels."

   d. "To deny me my right to eat Double Whoppers and Ultimate Cheeseburgers as I sit behind the golden EIB microphones."

   e. "To have dogs, cats, werewolves, squirrels, elephants, rhinos, and pigs take over downtown Washington. Actually, that's not such a bad idea."

80. According to Rush, "More people have died _____ than have died in nuclear power accidents."

   a. from broken condoms

   b. in Sarajevo

   c. from listening to the Larry King show

   d. at Chappaquiddick

   e. from voting for Michael Dukakis

81. What group did Rush call "a terrorist organization"?

   a. the Palestine Liberation Organization

   b. the National Organization for Women

   c. the Democratic party

   d. the Black Panthers

   e. the National Rifle Association

82. Rush made the following statement: "And do _____ pay anything back? Do they contribute taxes? No. They don't pay a thing. They contribute nothing to this country. They do nothing but take from it."

   a. lawyers

   b. multinational corporations

   c. Mexicans

   d. left-wing actresses

   e. the poor

83. Match the following terms from "the politically correct liberal lexicon" with their proper meanings:

a.	blasphemy	**1.**	mental illness
b.	right	**2.**	conservatives
c.	suburbs	**3.**	wrong
d.	homophobia	**4.**	*Heather Has Two Mommies*
e.	Good Book	**5.**	saying anything critical about Mother Earth
f.	Nazis	**6.**	dangerous bastions of racism

84. According to Rush, "A feminazi is a woman to whom the most important thing in life is _____."

   a. seeing to it that as many abortions as possible are performed

   b. the castration of all men

   c. the global liberation of women, regardless of how many men have to be killed

   d. trying to get my radio show off the air

   e. finding someone to have sex with

85. According to Rush, the real message of the "Murphy Brown" episode involving Dan Quayle and single motherhood was _____.

   a. "that left-wing women shouldn't be allowed to reproduce"

   b. "that Candice Bergen can't act"

   c. "that Dan Quayle is on the cutting edge of societal evolution"

   d. "that there are feminazis out there, demanding their right to abortion as the most important thing in their life"

   e. "that women don't need men, shouldn't desire them, and that total fulfillment and happiness can be achieved without men or husbands"

86. According to Rush, why was the feminist movement created?

   a. "to allow ugly women access to the mainstream of society"

   b. "to force all women to have abortions"

   c. "to attempt to overthrow the natural order of male domination"

   d. "to rebel against God—who is a man, by the way"

   e. "to make male lesbians more socially acceptable"

87. What did Rush say to a group of gay activists who had demonstrated inside St. Patrick's Cathedral in New York?

   a. "I feel your pain."

   b. "Hire some pervert homosexual to run a prostitution ring out of your condo, and they'll call you a genius."

   c. "Take your deadly, sickly behavior and keep it to yourselves."

   d. "May you all acquire Rock Hudson's disease."

   e. "When a gay person turns his back on you, it is anything but an insult; it's an invitation."

88. According to Rush, what was "new" about "the so-called 'New Left' of the 1960s"?

   a. "It was simply the tired old left dressed up in tie-dyed shirts, sandals, and granny glasses."

   b. "These turkeys finally figured out that Mao was right—the basis of political power is the barrel of a gun."

   c. "Sex, drugs, and rock and roll."

   d. "They attempted to purchase nuclear weapons from China."

   e. "No member of the 'Old Left' ever used a condom."

89. Which three events does Rush suggest for the "Homeless Olympics"?

   a. the ten-meter shopping cart relay

   b. the dumpster dig

   c. the soup can toss

   d. the cardboard box luge

   e. the hop, skip, and trip

90. A group of women who had won admission to an exclusive, all-male club demanded their own exercise room. According to Rush, how did the club respond?

a. They converted the building into a strip joint and invited the women to audition.

b. They equipped the exercise room with the latest in Nautilus equipment, but made the women dress in a hallway.

c. They placed a bed and a box of condoms in the women's restroom.

d. They required all users of the exercise room to prove they had appeared nude in *Playboy*.

e. They acceded to the women's demands and installed a washing machine, ironing board, and vacuum cleaner.

91. What is Rush's position on nuclear weapons?

a. "They're Republican instruments of death."

b. "There's only one way to get rid of nuclear arms—use 'em. All of 'em. Then there won't be anyone left to build more."

c. "The Evil Empire should be turned into a smoking, radiating ruin."

d. "The United States should invade Russia and confiscate their nuclear weapons."

e. "I'd like to have a few nukes of my own. Then liberals would finally show me some respect."

92. Which of the following statements about blacks did Rush *not* make?

   a. "Blacks on the 'Arsenio Hall Show' are angry, bitter, have angry frowns on their face and want to go out and burn every vestige of authority."

   b. "Why does the black community have to be heard? They're twelve percent of the population—who the hell cares?"

   c. "The NAACP should have riot rehearsal. They should get a liquor store and practice robberies."

   d. "Many black leaders are complacent slaves on the liberal plantation."

   e. "How come every black welfare mother you see at a grocery store has curlers in her hair and weighs 400 pounds?"

93. According to Rush, "The poorest people in America _____."

   a. are poor because they eat nothing but watermelon and barbecued ribs

   b. should rise up against the indignities of capitalist exploitation

   c. are the scum of the earth

   d. are better off than the mainstream families of Europe

   e. are all Democrats

94. What was Rush's response when asked about the fact that the NAFTA treaty could cause American jobs to go to Mexico?

  a. "Who cares? I'm set for life."

  b. "Hell if I know. Ask Ross Perot."

  c. "If you are unskilled and uneducated, your job is going south. Let stupid and unskilled Mexicans do that work."

  d. "Don't worry. No American corporation is going to move their operations to a country where everyone lives in boarded-up shacks and the drinking water is darker than shit."

  e. "The only thing that matters is that *Bill Clinton's* job is going south. Ha, ha, ha."

95. Rush made the following statement regarding American education: "Do you really think the situation in the schools would turn around if we threw more money at them? What would they do with it? _____."

  a. Buy condoms with even a greater variety of flavors and colors?

  b. Give raises to teachers who can't even read?

  c. Build on-site delivery rooms, so that pregnant schoolgirls don't have to miss their algebra quizzes?

  d. Buy guns for the white guys, so they can defend themselves against the black guys?

  e. Create inter-gender wrestling programs?

96. According to Rush, a vote for Clinton-Gore is
_____.

   a. "stupid"

   b. "the result of cocaine addiction"

   c. "a vote for socialism"

   d. "a vote for two guys with the phoniest southern accents I've ever heard"

   e. "a vote for a liberal, draft-dodging, Gennifer-loving, nihilistic, atheistic, anti-American member of the Me Generation"

97. According to Rush, how can the issue of women in the military be solved?

   a. by kicking women out of the military and providing them retraining in cooking and cleaning

   b. by forming 52 "PMS battalions" of women with the condition, led by "Sergeant Major" Molly Yard

   c. by placing women soldiers in a circle and arming them with automatic weapons

   d. by performing sex-change operations

   e. by placing them in units with gay men

98. Rush has made the following argument: "They say that kids are going to have sex, that we can't stop them. Therefore, they need protection. Hence, condoms." Which of the following "analogies" does Rush *not* draw from "this brilliant logic"?

   a. "Let's just admit that kids are going to do drugs and distribute safe, untainted drugs every morning in homeroom."

   b. "Kids are going to smoke, too, we can't stop them, so let's provide packs of low-tar cigarettes to the students for their after-sex smoke."

   c. "Kids will get guns and shoot them, you can't stop them, so let's give all the teachers bullet-proof vests."

   d. "If we are really concerned about safe sex, why stop at condoms? Let's convert study halls to Safe Sex Centers where students can go to actually have sex on nice double beds with clean sheets and under the watchful and approving eyes of the school nurse, who will be on hand to demonstrate, along with the principal, just how to use a condom."

   e. "Let's just make murder legal. No murderer in New York gets caught anyway. If we legalize it, the crime rate will go down, and everyone will feel safer."

99. What practice did Rush accuse liberals of supporting?

  a. abortion on the basis of sexual orientation

  b. mandatory sterilization for welfare recipients

  c. ten-year prison terms for anyone who criticizes Hillary Clinton

  d. sexual attacks on young girls in New York City swimming pools

  e. requiring members of the KKK to watch "Arsenio Hall"

100. What did Rush say about the peace movement?

  a. "Give it a chance."

  b. "Every one of those people is a Communist."

  c. "The peace movement has everything Bill Clinton likes: unwashed hair, treason, and free sex."

  d. "If they want to protest something, let them protest the wheel. It kills more people each year than nuclear bombs do."

  e. "They shouldn't call it the peace movement. They should call it the war movement. If these wimps succeed, we're sure to be invaded by Canada."

V. THE RUSH TO EXCELLENCE

"The Rush to Excellence" concerns Rush's career. Rush has the hottest radio show on the air, two best-selling books, a highly rated TV show, audiotapes, a massively profitable newsletter, mugs, T-shirts, bumper stickers, 900 numbers, fan clubs, "The Rush Limbaugh Morning Update" (a ninety-second radio commentary), and speaking engagements at more than $25,000 a pop. Hundreds of fans have paid $1,500 to take seminars on an ocean cruise with him. He sponsored the National Conservative Forum, which brought together various right-wing luminaries.

Rush's lifelong goal has been to be the best radio talk show host of all time. Indeed, no one has contributed more than Rush to the revitalization of AM radio (which he calls "the Limbaugh Effect"). On November 7, 1993, Rush was inducted into the Radio Hall of Fame of the Museum of Broadcast Communications. *People* magazine noted that Rush "has become a one-man carnival of right-wing rabble-rousing."

With all this, what more could Rush possibly do?

As it turns out, plenty. As many as three hundred restaurants across the fruited plain have established "Rush Rooms," so that dedicated dittoheads can gain weight and wisdom at the same time. Rush recommends hanging out at "Rush Rooms" as the best way to meet a like-minded member of the opposite sex.

Then there are dittohead conventions. On May 22, 1993, thirty thousand people showed up in Fort Collins, Colorado, for "Dan's Bake Sale," to help Dan Kay come up with the $29.95 necessary to subscribe to *The Limbaugh Letter*. (Not that he didn't actually have the money; it was just that his liberal wife wouldn't let him spend their money on Rush.)

Sometimes being Rush requires doing battle with the powers that be. Rush has quarreled with Congress over the proposed "Hush Rush" law (which would require stations to carry politically balanced programming). He also argued with the Armed Forces Radio Network over their initial refusal to carry his show.

Rush was even the subject of a short-lived sitcom. In 1994, the "Monty" program debuted on the Fox television network. Henry Winkler played a pompous radio talk show host who was surrounded by disrespectful liberals. Rush protested that the "Monty" character was not based on him, since he comes home to a small solitary apartment rather than a palacial house, and since he's not married to a liberal nag. Rush expressed pleasure at the fact that the show was canceled due to poor ratings.

Rush has also entered the world of acting. In April 1994, he appeared as himself on "Hearts Afire" (which is produced by Linda Bloodworth-Thomason, a close friend of Bill and Hillary Clinton). Rush's persona was warm, gracious, and charming as he wooed a married, liberal journalist.

This section of the quiz tests your intimate familiarity with Rush's TV and radio shows, the "Rush to Excellence" tour, and *The Limbaugh Letter*—matters that are all vital to the national security of the United States.

101. What did a reviewer for the *New York Times* have to say about Rush's book *The Way Things Ought to Be*?

a. "Deserves a place between Plato and Socrates on every thinking person's bookshelf."

b. "A rant of opinions, gags, and insults, with a few facts or near-facts sprinkled in like the meat in last week's stew."

c. "What a joke. Where did this guy go to school? And to think that millions of trees gave their life for this."

d. "I'm surprised that Mr. Limbaugh's ego was able to fit on the page.

e. "I would rename this book *The Way Things Aren't, Never Were, and Should Never Be*."

102. Who is listed as the "head writer" on Rush's television show?

a. Rush Limbaugh

b. William Shakespeare

c. Bill Clinton

d. Conan O'Brien

e. Tom Wolfe

103. How did a patron of the "Rush Room" at Blackie's House of Beef in Washington, D.C., describe the experience?

  a. "It's enough to make you barf."

  b. "Even better than spending spring break in Palm Beach with Ted Kennedy."

  c. "It's awesome. You fill up your stomach and your brain at the same time. I always come out feeling like a zombie."

  d. "It's reassuring to know that Rush is out there protecting you, and he goes great with red meat. This is Muzak for right-wing dining."

  e. "The dittoburger could have used more salt."

104. Bill Clinton plays "Taxula" in a mock commercial on Rush's radio show. How does Rush describe the character?

  a. "He sleeps in the daytime and has been known to prowl at night."

  b. "He loves to suck the living blood out of you."

  c. "Even scarier than his sidekick, 'Algore.'"

  d. "He lies, he cheats, he inhales."

  e. "He does nothing without the approval of his female master, 'Hillary the Vampire.'"

105. What is the theme music for Rush's radio show?

a. Snap, "I Got the Power"

b. Tracy Chapman, "Talking About a Revolution"

c. the Pretenders, "My City Was Gone"

d. Fleetwood Mac, "Tell Me Lies"

e. Blondie, "Call Me!"

f. Aretha Franklin, "R-E-S-P-E-C-T"

g. Elvis Presley, "Ain't Nothing But a Hounddog"

h. Garth Brooks, "Friends in Low Places"

i. Michael Jackson, "Thriller"

j. Gloria Gaynor, "I Will Survive"

106. What was the headline of the supermarket tabloid *Weekly World News* of April 19, 1994?

a. "Rush Limbaugh Has Biggest Brain in Universe!"

b. "Rush Limbaugh Born of Virgin Birth!"

c. "Rush Limbaugh Meets with Space Aliens!"

d. "Rush Limbaugh Balloons to 800 Pounds!"

e. "Rush Limbaugh the Reincarnation of Sigmund Freud!"

107. How did a mock commercial on Rush's radio show parody the Los Angeles riots?

- **a.** It offered a discount on the "Stealth bomber hand-gun," which goes undetected by police defenses.

- **b.** It offered an inflatable Rodney King doll, along with a police baton.

- **c.** It promoted "South Central Pawn Shop," which offered top dollar for merchandise that customers could prove was stolen from white-owned stores.

- **d.** It advertised the services of Damien Williams, who promised to incite a riot to protest the conviction of any black criminal.

- **e.** It offered mail-order bricks to be used as rioters' weapons.

108. In 1992, what song would Rush play on his radio show every time Ross Perot's name was mentioned?

    a. "When Johnny Comes Marching Home"

    b. Elton John, "The Bitch Is Back"

    c. "When the Saints Come Marching In"

    d. Patsy Cline, "Crazy"

    e. Randy Newman, "Short People"

109. Which two of the following are *not* regular advertisers on Rush's radio show?

    a. Coors Beer

    b. Hooked on Phonics

    c. CompuServe

    d. True Value Hardware

    e. the National Rifle Association

    f. The United Negro College Fund

    g. the Florida Orange Growers Association

    h. Speed Spanish

    i. Snapple

110. What disclaimer does Rush offer at the beginning of his radio show?

a. "The views expressed here are not necessarily the views of the staff or management of this network. But they should be—and soon *will* be."

b. "If any of you compassion fascists, environmental wackos, and feminazis out there are offended by racism and homophobia—well, that's *your* problem."

c. "Advice to the squeamish! Coming up: a point-by-point dissection of John Wayne Bobbitt."

d. "Our phone number is 1-800-282-2882. Don't bother to call if you're not a dittohead."

e. "This program is addictive. Millions of Americans have tested positive for EIB. Pretty soon your skull will be full of right-wing mush."

111. What is Rush's perspective on the "Fairness Doctrine"?

   a. "If people want to watch Pee-Wee Herman instead of me, who am I to stop them?"

   b. "Fairness? Fairness? Is *liberalism* fair?"

   c. "I don't need to be balanced with equal time. I *am* equal time."

   d. "Who cares? I can't be stopped! I will soon be on every radio station in the universe.

   e. "Fairness is not one of the thirty-five undeniable truths of life."

112. How did Rush celebrate "Earth Day" on his radio show?

   a. He conducted the program from the backseat of his limousine as he was driven aimlessly around New Jersey.

   b. He handed out styrofoam cups and plastic bags at a Burger King in Greenwich, Connecticut.

   c. He opened a chain of toxic waste dumps in Alabama.

   d. He hired a pilot to start fires in Yellowstone National Park.

   e. He played a tape of a chain saw cutting down a tree.

113. How did Rush open the first episode of his TV show?

   a. He demanded that every member of his studio audience sign a loyalty oath.

   b. He had G. Gordon Liddy fire a machine gun at a target with a picture of Bill Clinton.

   c. He conducted interviews with seven women who claim to have slept with Anita Hill.

   d. He had a blue dot superimposed on his face to protect his anonymity, because "I stand accused of being one of the most dangerous Americans alive today."

   e. He pleaded with viewers to call 1-800-THE-RUSH to order *The Way Things Ought to Be*.

114. Match the theme song to each of Rush's "Updates."

a.	Andy Williams, "Born Free"	**1.**	Pee-Wee Herman Update
b.	Clarence "Frogman" Henry, "Ain't Got No Home"	**2.**	Peace Update
c.	Dionne Warwick, "I'll Never Love This Way Again"	**3.**	AIDS Update
d.	Frankie Valli, "My Eyes Adored You"	**4.**	Animal Rights Update
e.	Slim Whitman, "Una Paloma Blanca"	**5.**	Gorbachev Update
f.	"Movin' On Up" (theme to "The Jeffersons")	**6.**	Carol Mosely Braun Update
g.	The Fifth Dimension, "Up, Up, and Away"	**7.**	Sexual Harassment Update
h.	theme from "The Empire Strikes Back"	**8.**	Barney Frank Update
i.	Millie Small, "My Boy Lollipop"	**9.**	Condom Update
j.	Michael Jackson, "Beat It"	**10.**	Homeless Update

115. Who has *not* been a guest on Rush's radio show?

a. George Bush

b. Pat Buchanan

c. Jesse Helms

d. Oliver North

e. Dan Quayle

116. How did a reporter who accompanied Rush on one of his weekend "Rush to Excellence" tours describe the experience?

a. "His control of the audience was masterful—and scary. He reminded me of Hitler."

b. "Never have I been so enlightened by a speaker. I would follow him anywhere."

c. "Women kept throwing themselves at him. It was incredible. He has more charisma than Jack Kennedy."

d. "The man is full of hate."

e. Within several hours, Rush had a hot dog, a box of popcorn, three cans of soda, a corned-beef sandwich, potato salad, pie, crackers, cookies, and chocolate mints, followed by a pass at the salad bar.

117. Which of the following is *not* an actual review of Rush's TV show?

a. "His compulsive self-promotion is more endearing than egregious."

b. "To succeed, the shiny-faced Spanky McFarland look-alike will have to do something more than sit there and complain about multiculturalists and feminazis."

c. "One must conclude that Limbaugh is the lead component of an insidious left-wing conspiracy to make conservatives look like clowns."

d. "It's almost enough to make me burn my television."

e. "The whole thing comes across about as real as the fat-free cheese and imitation butter whose commercials pay for the show."

f. "As disjointed and inept a half hour as TV offers."

g. "He woos the camera like an avid freshman on a date with the senior prom queen. He guffaws, he blusters, he bats his eyes, he makes kissy face. He will do anything to keep you watching."

h. "Like being stuck at a very bad party next to a disingenuously argumentative loudmouth who won't shut up even when his mouth is full of cheese dip."

i. "A nakedly exposed blowhard."

118. Which of the following statements has Rush *not* used to describe *The Limbaugh Letter?*

   a. "highly penetrating, incisive, and insightful"

   b. "my stellar publication"

   c. "your literary companion in times of trouble and tumult"

   d. "my sizzling journal of opinion"

   e. "even better than my best-selling books, *The Way Things Ought to Be* and *See, I Told You So*"

119. Which of the following T V shows did Rush *not* audition for?

   a. substitute host on "Pat Sajak"

   b. conservative counterpart to Mark Shields on "The MacNeil-Lehrer Newshour"

   c. a call-in show on CNN, à la Larry King

   d. a remake of "To Tell the Truth"

   e. a pilot for a show with Gloria Allred, entitled tentatively "Talk Wrestling"

120. What was Rush's "proud announcement" in the first issue of *The Limbaugh Letter*?

a. "This newsletter is printed on non-recycled paper. A grateful nation acknowledges the countless trees eager to sacrifice their sweet virgin pulp to support my words."

b. "Not a single uglo-American subscribes to this publication."

c. "I have now conquered every medium of communication known to man."

d. "This publication has already earned me $5 million. I am holding a check for that amount in my formerly nicotine-stained hands."

e. "I have just signed a contract to write my autobiography, *Just a Harmless Little Fuzzball*."

121. According to Rush, what is the chief purpose of his radio show?

a. "to impress women"

b. "to prepare the American people for the conservative revolution"

c. "to build and sustain such a large audience so I can charge advertisers confiscatory rates"

d. "to give federal bureaucrats something to listen to as they sit on their butts sharpening pencils and shuffling papers"

e. "to force radio stations in hick towns like Dubuque and Peoria to fire their afternoon disc jockeys"

122. What technique has Rush used to get rid of radio callers?

a. He interrupted them in mid-sentence with "What's the question? What's the question?"

b. He started singing "The Party's Over."

c. He went to a commercial for feminazi trading cards.

d. He performed "caller abortions," featuring the sound of a vacuum cleaner and a woman's scream.

e. He started yelling, "What sort of lesbo wacko Commie nut are you? Who let you on the air?"

123. How does Rush often begin his radio show?

a. "On sale now, exclusively through EIB: Bungee condoms, now available in the handy eighteen-pack Kennedy Saturday Night Special. Call 1-800-282-2882."

b. "Greetings, conversationalists across the fruited plain, this is Rush Limbaugh, the most dangerous man in America, with the largest hypothalamus in North America, serving humanity simply by opening my mouth, destined for my own wing in the Museum of Broadcasting, executing everything I do flawlessly with zero mistakes, doing this show with half my brain tied behind my back, just to make it fair because I have talent on loan from . . . God. Rush Limbaugh. A man. A legend. A way of life."

c. "This is Rush Limbaugh, here to explain the thirty-five undeniable truths of life and to bring pain and suffering to the arts-and-croissants crowd, environ-mental wackos, tree huggers, feminazis, multicul-turalists, and homeless activists. You are listening to the Excellence in Broadcasting Network, the patriotic center of the universe. EIB is an airborne phenomenon spread by casual contact, for which millions of Americans are testing positive."

d. "Greetings, dittoheads. This is your leader. Please suspend all critical thought for the next three hours."

e. "Welcome to another excursion into broadcast excellence. This is the poster boy of the American Dream. Coming up: attacks on Ted Kennedy, Hillary's husband, Ross Perot, the criminals' lobby, the onslaught of socialism, and . . . the . . . Reverend . . . Jackson. I am Rush Limbaugh, the turnpike of truth, ever clever, ever quick-witted, the only information highway you'll ever need, teaching the four Rs: reading, writing, arithmetic, and Rush."

124. Which of the following are Rush's improvised lyrics to "Born Free," by Andy Williams?

    a. "Eat beef! For beef is delicious! For beef is expensive! Rich peeeeeople love beeeeef!"

    b. "Born free or die! Born free or die!"

    c. "As free as the wind blows? Not under Clinton's taxation policies."

    d. "Watch out, Bambi—I've got a gun!"

    e. "Born free to follow your heart? Who has the time?"

125. What was the title of an article Rush wrote in *The Limbaugh Letter* on the Clinton health care plan?

    a. "Dr. Hillary: A Pain in the Butt"

    b. "Communism Comes to America"

    c. "Bend Over, America"

    d. "Rodhamized Medicine: New Age Mumbo-Jumbo and Liberal Psychobabble"

    e. "The Hillary Agenda: Bring on the Broccoli, Put Away the Cheetoes"

VI. RUSH ON RUSH

Rush Limbaugh seems to be a bundle of contradictions. On the one hand, he often comes across as the most egotistical man alive, referring to himself as "a profound success," "a legend, a way of life," "the passionate and sensitive Rush Limbaugh," and "the most dangerous man in America." On his radio show, Rush refers to his television show; on his television show, he refers to his radio show. On both shows, he refers to his books, his newsletter, and his speaking tours.

On the other hand, Rush mocks himself and refers to his "pompous arrogance shtick." Also, he admits that "my experiences with relationships have been less than sustaining in terms of happiness and contentment." He concedes that his relationship with his father was strained, and that he has tremendous difficulties controlling his weight.

He also has problems with self-esteem. Ever the narcissist, Rush told *Vanity Fair* in May 1992, "I have not changed a thing about my self-perception. I still get up and read the New York papers and see my name not mentioned and think I'm a failure, that I'm not mattering, that nobody knows who I am in the city I live in, and it bugs me greatly. I just sit here and get depressed."

Rush: we're here to help. For better or worse, we know who you are, we think you matter, and we don't think you're a failure. After all, how many people have a quiz book devoted to them? Cheer up!

The questions in this section explore what Rush has to say about himself—his fantasies, his self-descriptions, his philosophical agreement with Woody Allen, and his reason for remaining overweight. Maybe Rush will convince you that he's "just a harmless little fuzzball."

126. How does Rush assess his own maturity?

a. "You think I'm immature? Geez! What the hell are you saying? Get the hell out of here!"

b. "I still sweat bullets every time I talk to a woman who speaks in complete sentences."

c. "I gained 100 pounds the first year I was in New York. Does it *sound* like I'm well-adjusted?"

d. "I get up, I go to work, I pay my bills, I haven't slept with any Arkansas state troopers. Anything beyond that is icing on the cake."

e. "I'm just a kid. I haven't even grown up. I'm 42, but I feel like I'm still from the Midwest. I still feel like somebody 45 is my elder and that I've got to show them parental-type respect."

127. Why does Rush think he can't sustain a romantic relationship?

a. "No woman is good enough for me."

b. "I've never gotten over Mom."

c. "Every woman in New York is a lesbian or an environmental wacko."

d. "I'm too much in love with myself."

e. "I've heard you have to let them talk."

128. What is "the Limbaugh neutron bomb"?

   a. "It vaporizes liberals but leaves conservatives standing."

   b. Rush's name for his daily breakfast of three Big Macs, two chili dogs, and a twenty-four-inch pepperoni pizza

   c. "It neutralizes years of education at feminazi enclaves like Smith and Wellesley."

   d. "my mouth"

   e. "It inflicts massive retaliation on representatives of anticapitalism, multiculturalism, secular humanism, and socialism."

129. According to Rush, "I've never called anyone a _____ on the air."

   a. Gorbasmic dunce

   b. bitch

   c. racist

   d. pervert homosexual

   e. premenstrual terrorist

130. Which of the following phrases has Rush *not* used to describe himself?

   a. "the epitome of morality and virtue"

   b. "the Doctor of Democracy"

   c. "holder of the Attila the Hun Chair at the Limbaugh Institute for Advanced Conservative Studies"

   d. "the only healthful addiction in America"

   e. "almost as powerful as God Himself"

131. According to Rush, "Everyone is aware of my aversion to _____."

   a. women who don't know their place

   b. double bacon cheeseburgers

   c. self-promotion and braggadocio

   d. exercise of any kind

   e. Dan Rather and Peter Jennings

132. According to Rush, "Nice guys _____."

a. never get laid

b. finish last

c. are destined to inherit the earth

d. really bore me

e. don't belong in the Republican party

133. Why does Rush believe he remains over-weight?

a. "I am deeply insecure."

b. "Chocolate-covered Twinkies aren't just for breakfast anymore."

c. "Clinton's election threw me for an emotional tailspin."

d. "Liberal doctors in Kansas City injected me with substances designed to slow down my metabolism."

e. "I know any women pursuing me cannot be doing it for anything other than love."

134. What does Rush call a "fantasy"?

   a. "being tied up by Kim Basinger"

   b. "being elected president of the United States"

   c. "just having a relationship"

   d. "punching Jesse Jackson in the nose"

   e. "having my show on every radio station in the country"

135. On what critical point does Rush agree with Woody Allen?

   a. "Ninety-eight percent of life is just showing up."

   b. "All success means is that you get rejected by a higher class of women."

   c. "I wouldn't want to belong to any organization that would have me for a member."

   d. "Is sex dirty? Only if you do it right."

   e. "Getting through the night is becoming harder and harder. Last evening, I had the uneasy feeling that some men were trying to break into my room to shampoo me. But why?"

136. Why does Rush believe he is a "profound success"?

   a. "I relentlessly pursue the truth, and I do so with the epitome of accuracy."

   b. "The mass is an ass."

   c. "Who the hell wants to listen to Larry King?"

   d. "My throat is golden."

   e. "Millions of women spend their days fantasizing about me."

137. According to Rush, "As you people know, I seldom talk about _____."

   a. my four children

   b. my seven years at Leavenworth prison

   c. my deep-seated hostility to homosexuals

   d. myself

   e. uglo-American feminazi abortionists

138. According to Rush, "I am not _____."

a. a crook

b. a suitable husband for any woman

c. a racist, homophobe, male chauvinist pig, or any of that

d. a card-carrying member of the Democratic party, the ACLU, Common Cause, or any other Communist organization

e. an egomaniac

139. How does Rush believe historians will view the current epoch?

a. "the era of Limbaugh"

b. "the decade of greed"

c. "the Billary moment"

d. "the period of pain"

e. "the age of Madonna"

140. Which of the following characterizations has Rush *not* made of himself?

  a. "poster boy for the American way of life"

  b. "general all-around good guy"

  c. "lover of mankind"

  d. "protector of fatherhood"

  e. "epitome of chastity"

141. What did Rush do on his radio show to commemorate the thirtieth anniversary of John Kennedy's death?

  a. He ordered all callers to begin by revealing "where you were and what you were doing on the day when you first heard *me.*"

  b. He played a tape of Ted Kennedy's press conference following Chappaquiddick.

  c. He opened every hour with "Happy Days Are Here Again!"

  d. He read a list of American soldiers killed during the Bay of Pigs.

  e. He opened a special telephone line for women who slept with President Kennedy in the White House.

142. According to Rush, "I like the women's movement _____."

    a. just fine. Some of my best friends are women

    b. as long as they keep their mouths shut

    c. about as much as I like root canal

    d. from behind

    e. as long as it's run by women. Those people can't get anything straight

143. According to Rush, "My views on the environment are rooted _____."

    a. in the statements of Bo Snerdly, my call-screener, who says there's plenty of everything

    b. on a close reading of *Earth in the Lurch*, by Algore

    c. in my belief in Creation

    d. on my experiences snowmobiling across the Boundary Waters Canoe Area

    e. in a fourteen-hour conversation with James Watt

144. How many times did Rush say "I," "me," "myself," or "Rush Limbaugh" during a five-minute period on his radio program on April 27, 1993?

   a. 0

   b. 4

   c. 13

   d. 74

   e. 1,777,992

145. What did Rush say after his divorce from his first wife?

   a. "That's it, I'm through with women. I'm going to be asexual."

   b. "She's right. I *am* a pig."

   c. "Where's that Asian mail-order catalog?"

   d. "Does anyone have Madonna's phone number?"

   e. "It was like a horror movie—*I Was Married to a Feminazi!* The last few months, she kept yelling that sex is rape, and that she needed to get in touch with her 'inner bitch.'"

146. Why did Rush want to be a disc jockey at KGMO in Cape Girardeau at age 16?

a. "It was the only thing I could think of to impress this girl. Every day, I played 'I Want to Hold Your Hand' and dedicated it to her. She still refused to go out with me. I thought girls liked that sort of stuff."

b. "I loved music, plus I wanted to be popular."

c. "They let me out of gym class to do it. I hated having to learn the polka. Plus, playing dodgeball was awful. I was such a big target."

d. "It was the only thing I was good at. I didn't know much about history, about geography, about biology, or about trigonometry. I didn't know what a slide rule was for."

e. "I loved the sound of my own voice."

147. According to Rush, "I am a great _____."

a. softball player. I love playing left field

b. violinist. Calypso Louie Farrakhan has nothing on me

c. philanthropist. The NRA, the Tobacco Institute, the men's movement, the white supremacy movement— I've funded them all

d. boyfriend. I bring my dates to my radio show, my TV show, my speeches, and my interviews. I really show them a good time

e. kisser. The secret is out, that's the point of this. I don't need practice to be a good kisser

148. Which two of the following thoughts has Rush had on art and culture?

a. "How does this help me make money? What does it all mean? I don't get it."

b. "Did Michelangelo ever use the term knockers? I was just wondering."

c. "I don't go to museums because they don't have golf carts. If you put a golf cart in a museum, I'll go—you can drive around it a lot faster."

d. "Andy Warhol was wrong. My fame will last for fifteen *millennia*."

e. "Who needs all these paintings when you can listen to me?"

149. According to Rush, "If I had to describe myself in one word I would call myself a _____."

  a. meathead

  b. misogynist

  c. gadfly

  d. pseudo-intellectual

  e. comedian

150. According to Rush, "One of my biggest thrills in life was when I learned that _____."

  a. the Berlin Wall had fallen

  b. Crystal Bernard was interested in me

  c. my IQ is higher than Dan Quayle's

  d. Tom Clancy listens to me

  e. Roger Clinton was getting married

VII. FRIENDS AND ENEMIES

Nearly everyone has an opinion on Rush Limbaugh. Millions of his listeners fall over themselves expressing "mega-dittoes." President Bush carried Rush's bags when he stayed overnight at the White House. At "Dan's Bake Sale," scores of young men painted "Rush is God" on their backs.

But Rush has plenty of enemies, too—especially liberals, gays, feminists, Democrats, and blacks. A feminist in Kansas City called Rush "a harmless nut." There's even a newsletter devoted exclusively to bashing Rush (*The Flush Rush Quarterly*). William Raspberry, a columnist for the *Washington Post*, was appalled to discover that Rush had praised one of his columns on the air. During the 1992 campaign, Hillary Clinton erupted into sustained laughter upon hearing Rush's name. Gloria Allred, a feminist lawyer in Los Angeles, says, "I don't want to compare him to Hitler. But I will say that I wish Hitler had been taken more seriously in the beginning."

Peter J. Boyer, in *Vanity Fair,* had all sorts of things to say about Rush. In a May 1992 profile, he called Rush "talk radio's bombast king," "the patron saint of white male chauvinists," "the secret weapon of the Republican rebellion," and "the court jester of the disaffected politically incorrect."

Of course, Rush has friends as well as enemies. William F. Buckley, Rush's fellow right-wing traveler, says that Rush is "like a jolt of champagne for most of us, reorienting the day, reassuring us that social disorders haven't disturbed the essential movements of the planets."

From Larry King to Ralph Nader, from Oliver North to Ted Koppel, from Howard Stern to *MAD* magazine— everyone's talking about Rush. And after answering 150 questions about the guy, you understand why.

151. Match the individual with their pronunciation of "Rush Limbaugh":

a.	"Russ"	**1.**	Rush Limbaugh
b.	"Lim-bough," as in "Ow! That hurts"	**2.**	George Bush
c.	"Limbo"	**3.**	William F. Buckley
d.	"Rush (hear him while he's hot) Limbaugh (as in 'awe')"	**4.**	Hillary Rodham Clinton

152. What did Howard Stern say about Rush?

a. "Rush owes me a lot. I feed that big fat head of his."

b. "I begged that guy to endorse me for governor, and he blew me off."

c. "I'm gonna drive him off the air."

d. "I hate egotistical men."

e. "Rush's foreign policy experience is pretty much confined to having breakfast once at the International House of Pancakes."

153. What award did Rush receive from *MAD* magazine?

a. "easiest American to make fun of"

b. "looks most like Alfred E. Newman"

c. "most deserving of unnecessary root canal work"

d. "biggest blow-hard since George Wallace"

e. "most cherubic face in American radio"

154. What did Jay Leno say about "Dan's Bake Sale," which drew thirty thousand "dittoheads" to Fort Collins, Colorado, in 1993?

a. "Should Rush really be eating baked goods?"

b. "Don't they have laws in Fort Collins against unnecessary assembly?"

c. "Why didn't the Democrats just drop a bomb on the place?"

d. "I know the prison overcrowding problem is serious, but this is ridiculous! Who are they going to let out next?"

e. "A conservative Woodstock? I mean, the last time that many conservatives got together I think it was in Berlin, about 1933."

155. According to a 1993 poll, which two of the following individuals would Americans most like to say, "Oh, shut up" to?

a. Rush Limbaugh

b. Ross Perot

c. Pat Buchanan

d. Louis Farrakhan

e. Jesse Jackson

156. What do Rush Limbaugh, Anita Bryant, and Burt Reynolds have in common?

a. They've all been in love with Loni Anderson.

b. They all like to tame alligators in the Florida Keys.

c. They've all been spokesmen for the Florida Citrus Commission.

d. They've all organized antiwar demonstrations in London.

e. They all voted for Pat Robertson for president.

157. In March 1994, upward of ten thousand ditto-heads showed up at the Madera County (California) Fairgrounds. Which three of the following took place?

    a. They conducted an Al Gore tree hugging contest.

    b. They served barbecued "spotted owl."

    c. They sold T-shirts with the slogan, "Inhale to the Chief."

    d. They refused entrance to anyone named "Kennedy."

    e. They paid G. Gordon Liddy to walk barefoot over a bed of hot coals.

158. What does the publisher of *Flush Rush Quarterly* have to say about Rush?

    a. "A man of deeply held values and moral purpose."

    b. "I love Rush. He's my meal ticket."

    c. "He's the voice of Middle America."

    d. "A right-wing kook."

    e. "He's a pot-smoking, draft-dodging, homophobic, sexist, racist clown prince of the airwaves who is a danger to our environment, the animal population, and free-thinking people everywhere."

159. In February 1994, Ronald Gene Barbour, a forty-five-year-old unemployed limousine driver from Orlando, was arrested on a charge of threatening to kill President Clinton. What did Barbour say from his jail cell?

    a. "My sincerest apologies. How could I have gone so astray?"

    b. "I like Rush, I sure do. I love his polemics on Clinton. He's a disgrace to this country. He should be where I am. He's a public enemy."

    c. "I was hired by Al Gore."

    d. "Just joking."

    e. "I was simply expressing my rights under the first and second amendments. It's a sad day in this country when the federal government takes away your liberties."

160. According to Larry King, what book will Rush *not* be writing?

    a. *The Democrats and the Communist Party: None Dare Call It Treason*

    b. *My Rush to Excellence: The Greatest Story Ever Told*

    c. *Diary of a Rock and Roll Republican*

    d. *Oppression, Bigotry, Racism: America's Legacy*

    e. *See, I Keep Telling You So!*

161. In his debate with Ross Perot on "Larry King Live," what did Al Gore call Rush?

   a. "a distinguished American"

   b. "a threat to the republic"

   c. "a tree mugger"

   d. "a menace to the Democratic party"

   e. "someone that Tipper has taken quite a liking to; it's causing a real strain in our marriage"

162. Which of the following characteristics does Rush *not* share with Howard Stern?

   a. Both were born on January 12.

   b. Both had overbearing fathers who made them feel like misfits.

   c. Both work in midtown Manhattan.

   d. Both are Snapple spokesmen.

   e. Both have run for political office.

163. Which of the following characteristics does the American public think best applies to Rush?

   a. intelligent

   b. obnoxious

   c. tells it like it is

   d. offensive

   e. has a cruel and juvenile sense of humor

   f. demeaning to women

   g. demeaning to blacks and other minorities

   h. irresponsible

164. How did a caller to Rush's radio show describe Rush's physique?

   a. "pretty good for a male lesbian"

   b. "Arnold Swarzennager, times two"

   c. "a real turn-on"

   d. "horizontally gifted"

   e. "a big white elephant"

165. What did Ronald Reagan write to Rush in December 1992?

a. "Would you please tell Ollie North to stop lying about Iran-contra?"

b. "Rush, we agree on one thing: George Bush is a real wimp."

c. "Now that I've retired, I don't mind that you've become the number one voice for conservatives in the country."

d. "Nancy is in love with you."

e. "What was your name again?"

166. Political humorist Art Buchwald made the following statement: "I don't think that Rush knows *anything* about _____."

a. Puerto Rico

b. *anything*

c. power tools

d. the G-spot

e. orange juice

167. When Rush appeared as himself on "Hearts Afire," he captivated one of the female characters. She said to herself, "This is Rush Limbaugh we're talking about. It's like being attracted to _____."

a. Bobby Knight

b. Richard Nixon

c. Cheech and Chong

d. Michael Jackson

e. Tom Arnold

168. In a poll of one thousand registered voters in July 1993, what was the most-cited reason why people listen to Rush's radio show?

a. "He gives better information on the issues."

b. "He represents their views."

c. "I'm hoping to bear his children."

d. "Larry King is just too damn rude."

e. "He is fun and entertaining."

169. What is the favorite bumper sticker of "dittoheads"?

a. "Rush Is Right"

b. "Sex, Drugs, and Rush"

c. "Rush Is God"

d. "Rush—Rock On"

e. "Limbaugh and Cocaine: What a Rush!"

170. In a poll of one thousand registered voters in July 1993, which person had the *lowest* public approval rating?

a. Oprah Winfrey

b. Ross Perot

c. Bill Clinton

d. Rush Limbaugh

e. Phil Donahue

171. Who called Rush "Rush Slimebaugh"?

a. Phyllis Diller

d. Hillary Clinton

c. Miss Manners

d. Erma Bombeck

e. Bob Dole

172. What did Ted Koppel say about Rush?

a. "To the left, he's like an aching tooth."

b. "I don't like his hair."

c. "A very impressive guy. He's the smartest college dropout I've ever met."

d. "He's promised to name me his secretary of state."

e. "He's great to go bar-hopping with. We do our imitations of Howard Cosell and Ross Perot all night long."

173. Who called Rush "probably our greatest living American"?

   a. Al Sharpton

   b. William Bennett

   c. Robert Bork

   d. Lyndon LaRouche

   e. Clarence Thomas

174. What did Oliver North say about Rush?

   a. "He's so big he needs his own zip code."

   b. "A human handkerchief."

   c. "A big, fat dope. Rush's mom named him that because he was always rushing to the fridge."

   d. "I'm amazed that somebody named Rush would have such a slow metabolism."

   e. "Gay-bashing, bashing women, 'feminazis,' bashing blacks—I don't think that's funny."

175. What two things did David Letterman say to Rush during his appearance on "Late Show"?

    a. "You're the finest-looking human specimen on this planet."

    b. "What are the top ten reasons you hate Hillary Clinton?"

    c. "My Mom's much hipper than yours."

    d. "George Bush or Dan Quayle—who's the bigger pinhead?"

    e. "Do you ever wake up in the middle of the night and just think to yourself, 'I'm so full of hot gas'?"

Answers and Their Sources

1. e   Steven V. Roberts, "What a Rush!" *US News and World Report*, August 16, 1993, p.31.

2. d   "ESPN SportsCenter: Sunday Conversation," April 3, 1994.

3. b   Michael Arkush, *Rush!* (New York: Avon Books, 1993), p.105.

4. b   *Rush!*, p. 2. (Jeff Christie is the on-air name Rush used at radio stations in Pittsburgh.)

5. c   John Patrick Zmirak, "I *Am* the Product," *Success*, June 1993, p.30.

6. d   Rush Limbaugh, *The Way Things Ought to Be* (New York: Pocket Books, 1992) p.17.

7. a   Paul D. Colford, *The Rush Limbaugh Story: Talent on Loan from God* (New York: St. Martin's Press, 1993), p.10.

8. c   *Rush!*, p.19.

9. a   *The Rush Limbaugh Story*, p.41.

10. b   "The Playboy Interview: Rush Limbaugh," *Playboy*, December 1993, p.74.

11. b   John McCollister, "The Rush is On," *The Saturday Evening Post*, May/June 1993, p.74.

12. e   *The Rush Limbaugh Story*, p.6; and Lewis Grossberger, "The Rush Hours," *The New York Times Magazine*, December 16, 1990, p.93. (Larry Lujak is a disc jockey at WLS in Chicago.)

13. c   *Rush!*, p.13.

14. d   *Rush!*, p.147.

15. e   *Rush!*, p.127.

16. a   *The Rush Limbaugh Story*, p.46.

17. c   *Rush!*, p.71.

18. a   *Rush!*, p.172.

19. d   Peter J. Boyer, "Bull Rush," *Vanity Fair*, May 1992, p.205.

20. e   *Vanity Fair*, May 1992, p.205.

21. d   *The Rush Limbaugh Story*, p.32. Rush is a graduate of the Elkin Institute of Radio and Technology, in Dallas.

22. c   *Rush!*, p.71. (Rush actually made the statement in answer e. See *Vanity Fair*, May 1992, p.204.)

23. e   Richard Corliss, "Conservative Provocateur or Big Blowhard?" *Time*, October 26, 1992, p.78.

24. b   *The Rush Limbaugh Story*, p.45.

25. a   *The Rush Limbaugh Story*, pp.4–5.

26. a   *US News and World Report*, August 16, 1993, p.35.

27. e   *US News and World Report*, August 16, 1993, p.31.

28. c   Mervyn Rothstein, "Rush's Judgment," *Cigar Aficionado*, Spring 1994, p.55.

29. d   Kurt Anderson, "Mr. Big Mouths," *Time*, November 1, 1993, p.65.

30. a, d, e Maureen Dowd, "A Shy, Sensitive Guy Trying to Get by in Lib City," *The New York Times*, March 24, 1993, p.C10.

31. e   *Rush!*, p.209.

32. a   *The Way Things Ought to Be*, p.108.

33. b   "20/20," November 5, 1993.

34. e   *Rush!*, p.210.

35. c   James Raia, "The King of the Right Wing," *Sacramento Magazine*, May 1988, p.64.

36. b   *Rush!*, p.42.

37. e   *The Rush Limbaugh Story*, p.164.

38. d   *The Rush Limbaugh Story*, p.xi.

39. c   *The Rush Limbaugh Story*, p.40.

40. c   *The Rush Limbaugh Story*, p.14.

41. e   Rush Limbaugh, *See, I Told You So* (New York: Pocket Books, 1993), p.10.

42. b   *Rush!*, p.69.

43. d   *Rush!*, p.78.

44. e   *Rush!*, p.124.

45. b   *The Rush Limbaugh Story*, p.92.

46. e   *The Rush Limbaugh Story*, p.103.

47. a   *Vanity Fair*, May 1992, p.207.

48. b   *Cigar Aficionado*, Spring 1994, p.47.

49. c   "Hearts Afire," April 11, 1994.

50. c   *The Rush Limbaugh Story*, p.220.

51. e   *Rush!*, p.184.

52. b   *Success*, June 1993, p.28.

53. e   **a:** Robert L. Bartley, "To the Ramparts of Populism: Ross, Rush & Us," *The Wall Street Journal*, September 23, 1993, p.16.
b: *See, I Told You So*, p.35.
c: *The Wall Street Journal*, September 23, 1993, p.16
d: Rush Limbaugh, "Get Angry, Bush," *The New York Times*, October 15, 1992, p.A27.

54. c   Mark Goodman, "Rush Limbaugh: Love Him or Loathe Him, He's the Most Provocative Voice on the Air," *People*, October 19, 1992, p.109.

55. d   Richard Corliss, "A Man. A Legend. A What!?" *Time*, September 23, 1991, p.66.

56. a   *Time*, September 23, 1991, p.66.

57. e   *Rush!*, p.210.

58. d   *The Way Things Ought to Be*, p.127.

59. a   *See, I Told You So*, p.160.

60. b   **a:** *Flush Rush Quarterly*, Fall 1993, p.12.
c: *The New York Times*, October 15, 1992, p.A27.
d: "From the Desk of Rush Limbaugh, Editor in Chief" (advertisement for *The Limbaugh Letter*, 1994)
e: *See, I Told You So*, p.44.

61. e   *The Way Things Ought to Be*, p.138.

62. a.4   *See, I Told You So*, p.40.
  b.6   *See, I Told You So*, p.40.
  c.10   *The Rush Limbaugh Story*, p.215.
  d.3   *The Rush Limbaugh Story*, p.133.
  e.5   *See, I Told You So*, p.40.
  f.9   *See, I Told You So*, p.161.
  g.8   *Time*, October 26, 1992, p.76.
  h.7   "Rush Limbaugh: The Television Show," November 22, 1993.
  i.1   *Time*, November 1, 1993, p.65.
  j.2   *Time*, November 1, 1993, p.65.

63. d   *The Rush Limbaugh Story*, p.52.

64. c   *Rush!*, pp.80–81.

65. e   *The Way Things Ought to Be*, p.292.

66. a   *See, I Told You So*, p.25.

67. a   **b:** *See, I Told You So*, p.144.
  c: *See, I Told You So*, p.253.
  d: *See, I Told You So*, p.143.
  e: "Rush Limbaugh: The Television Show," November 23, 1993.

68. c   *The Rush Limbaugh Story*, p.52.

69. b   *The Rush Limbaugh Story*, p.89.

70. a   *The Rush Limbaugh Story*, p.194.

71. e   Leslie Savan, "Sitting Here in Limbaugh," *Village Voice*, December 29, 1992, p.51.

72. c   *Success*, June 1993, p.30.

73. d   *The Limbaugh Letter*, June 1993, p. 2. Rush also said, "Charles, I really love you" (p.4).

74. b   Joshua Hammer, "Welcome to Rush's World," *Newsweek*, September 28, 1992, p.50.

75. c   Opening to "The Rush Limbaugh Show," every program, beginning of every hour.

76. d   "Hearts Afire," April 11, 1994.

77. e   Eric Morgenthaler, "'Dittoheads' All Over Make Rush Limbaugh Superstar of the Right," *The Wall Street Journal*, June 28, 1993, p.A10.

78. a   *Time*, September 23, 1991, p.66.

79. b   *Time*, September 23, 1991, p.66.

80. d   *Rush!*, p.88.

81. b   *Rush!*, p.131.

82. e   *The Way Things Ought to Be*, p.41.

83. a.5   *See, I Told You So*, p.313.
      b.3   *See, I Told You So*, p.321.
      c.6   *See, I Told You So*, p.322.
      d.1   *See, I Told You So*, p.318.
      e.4   *See, I Told You So*, p.317.
      f.2   *See, I Told You So*, p.319.

84. a   *The Way Things Ought to Be*, p.194.

85. e   *The Way Things Ought to Be*, p.189.

86. a   *The Rush Limbaugh Story*, p.89.

87. c   *The Rush Limbaugh Story*, p.109.

88. a   *See, I Told You So*, p.34.

89. a, b, e   *Rush!*, p.201.

90. e   *Rush!*, p.207.

91. b   *The Rush Limbaugh Story*, p.89.

92. e   **a, b, c:** *Flush Rush Quarterly*, Fall 1993, p.8.
          d: *Flush Rush Quarterly*, Spring 1993, p.3.

93. d   *Flush Rush Quarterly*, Spring 1993, p.3.

94. c   *Flush Rush Quarterly*, Fall 1993, p.6.

95. a   David Remnick, "Radio Free Limbaugh: He's Funny, But His Demagoguery Has a Dark Side," *Washington Post National Weekly Edition*, February 28/March 6, 1994, p.24.

96. c   *Time*, October 26, 1992, p.76.

97. b   *Time*, October 26, 1992, p.78.

98. e   *Success*, June 1993, p.28.

99. d   *US News and World Report*, August 16, 1993, p.29.

100. d   *The Saturday Evening Post*, May/June 1993, p.54.

101. b   *Success*, June 1993, p.31.

102. c   *US News and World Report*, August 16, 1993, p.35.

103. d   "Off the Cuff: Steak *au* Limbaugh," *Gentleman's Quarterly*, October 1993, p.73.

104. a   *Cigar Aficionado*, Spring 1994, p.50.

105. c   *Cigar Aficianado*, Spring 1994, p.50.

106. c   "Rush Limbaugh Meets With Space Aliens! Historic Rendezvous Takes Place at Secret New Orleans Site," *Weekly World News*, April 19, 1994, p.1. The story reveals that "An official alien delegation from a planet outside our solar system has publicly backed popular talk show host Rush Limbaugh for President of the United States in the 1996 election." The aliens believe that "Bill Clinton" is too soft on criminals and has too many 'lawyer friends' to do much about a criminal justice system 'that is the joke of the universe.'" There are three picture of Rush with the aliens. One caption reads, "Historic meeting ends with a handshake. As is the custom on their planet, these aliens shake with their left hands" (p.8).

107. e   *Time*, November 1, 1993, p.64.

108. a   Terry Eastland, "Rush Limbaugh: Talking Back," *The American Spectator*, September 1992, p.24.

109. a, f   Edwin Diamond, "Roger & Me: Rush Comes to TV," *New York*, September 28, 1992, p.16; and *US News and World Report*, August 16, 1993, p.30.

110. a   *People*, October 19, 1992, p.109.

111. c   *People*, October 19, 1992, p.109.

112. e   *The Wall Street Journal*, June 28, 1993, p.1.

113. d *The Rush Limbaugh Story*, p.202.

114. a.4 *Rush!*, p.180; Joseph P. Kahn, "Talk Radio's Mr. Right," *The*
  b.10 *Boston Globe*, April 14, 1993, p.68; and *Time*, September 23,
  c.3 1991, p.65.
  d.7
  e.2
  f.6
  g.9
  h.5
  i.8
  j.1

115. c *Rush!*, p.216.

116. e *The Rush Limbaugh Story*, p.130.

117. d **a, b, c, e:** *The Rush Limbaugh Story*, p.204.
  f, g, h, i: *Rush!*, p.223.

118. e **a:** *The Limbaugh Letter*, September 1993, p.1.
  b: *The Limbaugh Letter*, October 1993, p.1.
  c: *The Limbaugh Letter*, May 1993, p.1.
  d: *The Limbaugh Letter*, August 1993, p.1.

119. b (Rush *volunteered* for the MacNeil-Lehrer commentator position, but was turned down.) *The Rush Limbaugh Story*, p.108.

120. a *The Limbaugh Letter*, October 1992, p.1.

121. c *Vanity Fair*, May 1992, p.204.

122. d James Bowman, "The Leader of the Opposition," *National
  Review*, September 6, 1993, p.48.

123. b *The American Spectator*, September 1992, p.23.

124. a *Vanity Fair*, May 1992, p.160.

125. c *The Limbaugh Letter*, November 1993, p.1.

126. e *US News and World Report*, August 16, 1993, p.35.

127. d *People*, October 19, 1992, p.112.

128. a   *Time*, September 23, 1991, p.65.

129. b   *Sacramento Magazine*, May 1988, p.160.

130. e

    a: *The Way Things Ought to Be*, p.301.
    b: *See, I Told You So*, p.18.
    c: "20/20," November 5, 1993.
    d: *The Way Things Ought to Be*, p.302.

131. c   *See, I Told You So*, p.25.

132. a   *Playboy*, December 1993, p.59.

133. e   *Vanity Fair*, May 1992, p.207.

134. c   *Vanity Fair*, May 1992, p.207.

135. b   *Playboy*, December 1993, p.76. The fifth quotation is from
Woody Allen, *Without Feathers* (New York: Random House,
1972), p.3.

136. a   *Playboy*, December 1993, p.78.

137. d   *The Limbaugh Letter*, October 1993, p.1.

138. c   *The Rush Limbaugh Story*, p.xii.

139. a   *The Limbaugh Letter*, front page, every issue.

140. e   *Cigar Aficianado*, Spring 1994, p.47.

141. a   "Rush Limbaugh," *People*, December 27, 1993, p.103.

142. d   *People*, October 19, 1992, p.109.

143. c   *The Way Things Ought to Be*, p.153.

144. d   *Flush Rush Quarterly*, Summer 1993, p.8.

145. a   *Rush!*, p.57.

146. b   *Vanity Fair*, May 1992, p.205.

147. e   *The Rush Limbaugh Story*, p.184.

148. b, c   Tom Tomorrow, "This Modern World" (cartoon), in *Flush Rush
Quarterly*, Spring 1994, p.7; and *Flush Rush Quarterly*, Spring
1994, p.12.

149. e   *Sacramento Magazine*, May 1988, p.64.

150. d   *The New York Times*, March 24, 1993, p.C10.

151. a.2
     b.4
     c.3
     d.1
                Time, October 26, 1992, p.76.

152. a   *Time*, November 1, 1993, p.63. (The fifth quotation is an actual statement, made by Pat Buchanan regarding Bill Clinton. See *The Rush Limbaugh Story*, p.180.)

153. c   "*MAD*'s Big Answer," *MAD* #322 (October 1993), p.3.

154. e   James Retter, "Good-Guy Leno Tells Some Mean Jokes," *The Los Angeles Times*, June 28, 1993, p. F3. The day after Leno told the joke, Rush grumbled on his radio show that he wasn't a Nazi and that his feelings were hurt; Jay called to apologize.

155. a, e   Ronald G. Shafer, "Washington Wire," *The Wall Street Journal*, October 29, 1993, p.1.

156. c   Larry Lohter, "Florida and Rush: Come on Down! The Controversy's Fine!" *The New York Times*, February 20, 1994, section 4, p.2.

157. a, b, c   "Limbaugh Legions Lambaste Lefties," *The Bakersfield Californian*, March 16, 1994, p.A6

158. e   Advertisement, *Flush Rush Quarterly*, 1994. Statement C is from Pat Buchanan, and is quoted in *Vanity Fair*, May 1992, p.204.

159. b   Lars-Erik Nelson, "Rush—Is His Venom Really Harmless?" *Liberal Opinion Week*, March 7, 1994, p.3.

160. d   "Larry King's People: News and Views," *USA Today*, March 21, 1994, p.4D.

161. a   "Excerpts From the Free Trade Debate Between Gore and Perot," *The New York Times*, November 10, 1993, p.B16. Gore put Rush in the same category as other "distinguished Americans" such as Colin Powell and Tip O'Neill.

162. e   *US News and World Report*, August 16, 1993, p.31; and *Time*, November 1, 1993, p.65.

163. a   *Time*, November 1, 1993, p. 62. The poll of 413 adult Americans who have heard or heard about Rush was taken on October 21, 1993 for *Time*/CNN by Yankelovich Partners, Inc. The results were as follows:

Which of these descriptions do you think apply to Rush Limbaugh?

Intelligent	71%
Obnoxious	66%
Tells it like it is	65%
Offensive	59%
Has a cruel and juvenile sense of humor	47%
Demeaning to women	41%
Demeaning to blacks and other minorities	34%
Irresponsible	33%

164. d   *Cigar Aficianado*, Spring 1994, p.47.

165. c   *US News and World Report*, August 16, 1993, p.30.

166. e   Art Buchwald, "Squeeze Me," *Liberal Opinion Week*, March 21, 1994, p.29.

167. b   "Hearts Afire," April 11, 1994.

168. e   *US News and World Report*, August 16, 1993, p.28.

169. a   *US News and World Report*, August 16, 1993, p.28.

170. d   *US News and World Report*, August 16, 1993, p.28.

171. d   *The Rush Limbaugh Story*, p.225.

172. a   "20/20," November 5, 1993.

173. b   *The American Spectator*, September 1992, p.23.

174. a   *The New York Times Magazine*, December 16, 1990, p.92. The other answers are actual statements, made by the following:
b: Ralph Nader: *The Rush Limbaugh Story*, p.169.
c: Howard Stern: *The Rush Limbaugh Story*, p.225.
d: Dennis Miller: *The Rush Limbaugh Story*, p.130.
e: Larry King: *The Rush Limbaugh Story*, p.174.

175. a, e   "Letterman Blasts Limbaugh," *Flush Rush Quarterly*, Spring 1994, p.10.

About the Author

Ted Rueter earned a Ph.D. in political science from the University of Wisconsin–Madison. He has taught at Middlebury College, Georgetown University, and Smith College. He lives in San Luis Obispo, California.

Rueter is the author of *Carter vs. Ford: The Counterfeit Debates of 1976, Teaching Assistant Strategies: An Introduction to College Teaching, The United States in the World Political Economy,* and *The Minnesota House of Representatives and the Professionalization of Politics.* His articles have appeared in the *New York Times,* the *Boston Globe, PS: Political Science and Politics, World Politics, The Journal of Politics, The Journal of Post-Keynesian Economics, Perspectives on Political Science,* and *Computerworld.*